Why Life Is Awful

Why Life Is Awful

David Hashioka

To order additional copies of this book, contact:
Xlibris
1-888-795-4274
www.Xlibris.com
Orders@Xlibris.com
717944

The technologically advanced alien beings can help humanity deal with its drinking water shortages, pollution problems, lumber shortages, spage age mineral supply problems, and truffle supply problems. The alien beings may help us determine what makes the resins used by Stradivarius in his musical instruments, so special. The alien beings will only help mankind if God permits it. God will permit the alien beings to help mankind if humanity does all it can to end poverty in the world. The wealthiest 8 countries in the world should share their wealth with the poorest 188 countries in the world. Only saints, angels, and avatars should be elected to high elected government positions. Since only they would have the courage to transfer the wealth from the world's richest people to the world's poorest people. 900 million people go hungry everyday. These people do not have the money to buy the food that they need. There is a severe shortage of lumber in the world today. In the United States, houses are being built from wood of 2-year old trees. During earlier times, new houses would only be constructed from lumber of 30-year old trees. More than 80% of the world's ancient old growth trees have been cut down. Lumber is so rare that no more mansions can be built for rich people. In many parts of the world people will be forced to live in cars, mobile homes and tents. Mankind must plant more lumber trees. More bricks must be used in the construction of new houses. Perhaps, new plastic boards can substitute for lumber in the construction of new houses. During Biblical times; many people lived in tents.

Humanity must avoid industrial agriculture as much as possible. Most of the crops in the United States is grown by industrial agriculture. Genetically modified seeds must not be used to grow crops. Chemical fertilizers should be used as little as possible. Use manure to fertilize crops. Crop rotation will reduce the need for fertilizer and pesticides. More than one crop should be grown at the same time on any farmland. By growing certain plants, pests can be greatly reduced. In areas of the world where water is limited in availability it would be wise to avoid growing crops that require a great deal of water to grow. According to Worldwatch Institute about 80% of the grain that is grown in the United States is used to feed livestock. It takes about 3 pounds of grain to produce 1 pound of chicken meat. It takes about 16 pounds of grain to produce 1 pound of steer beef. About 70% of agricultural land in the United States is used for the raising of livestock. In short, the less meat is produced, the more people can be fed with crops. It is alright to kill animals for food as long as the livestock is raised in a healthy environment and is killed with as little pain as possible. You should always thank God for all the food you eat. Many animals will only eat meat like dogs and cats. All pet dogs are sad that they can provide people with only temporary comfort of their friendship with their human companions. Pet dogs know that animals are much more forgiving at sinful humans than God is. God is too logical and too selfish to be as forgiving as he should be. God would value the love of humans more if he thought humans valued the love and friendship of strangers more. Even gangsters value their friends. But, do they treat strangers right. I think God believes most humans value material things more than people. God thinks most people are too selfish and that they are not very ethical. Recently, American voted to allow the Republicans to control both the United States House of Representatives and the United States Senate. Apparently the American Mafia had told the United States voters that the Godfathers would provide the American public with all the material things they wanted if they supported the Republican party. The most important freedom Americans have is not the ability to buy material goods and services. The most important freedom Americans have is to be able to criticize bad people. If you cannot hold bad people accountable for their sinful actions, democracy is badly affected. A free people cannot tolerate cruel people. Many celebrities have all the material things they want, but they are not happy people because the moment they became famous, they lost their freedom and their privacy. The moment you become famous, the Mafia assigns gangsters to watch your every move. These gangsters tell you who you can talk to and where you can go. These gangsters swat the bottoms of celebrities a lot. Celebrities have to take drugs or get drunk to deal with pain. I know that gangsters swat the bottoms of a lot of ethical people, because they swatted the bottoms of my father, my mother, my brother, and my sister. My relatives and many of my friends have been swatted as well. Rich Americans have been so successful at avoiding paying taxes that the United States federal government is so deeply in debt that the United States dollar is worth little. The droughts throughout the world will continue without the help of the alien beings. Environmental scientists have said that if the carbon dioxide level in the earth's atmosphere exceeded 350 parts per million, droughts would become a problem. Now, the carbon dioxide level in the earth's atmosphere has reached over 400 parts per million. The rain and snow will not return to many parts of the continental United States until we can get the approval of God and the alien beings. I know that the Godfather must help end world poverty by making himself poor if he wants God and the alien beings to help humanity. Apparently, Godfather does not want to impoverish himself in order to help mankind because he still wants to kill me. I spent 37 years of my life to gain knowledge on how to run the government and the world economy. If the Godfather kills me, he is going to lose all my wisdom. It will take the Godfather decades of reading to learn all the knowledge I know on how to run the government and the world economy. Apparently, the Godfathers think their egos are more important than the fate of humanity. The Godfathers gain more pleasure from making other people miserable than living free from the physical pain of hell. Without water, the agricultural land of the United States is worthless. Most of the land in the continental United States will become desert, over enough time. Most of the earth's land will become desert. By the years from 2025-2035 half of mankind (3.5 billion people) will be in dire need of water, according to many environmental scientists. Water is the key ingredient in many American products. As the price of water increases, Americans will have less money to buy things other than food. The less water there is, the more people will lose their jobs. People who clean swimming pools will lose their jobs. Many gardeners will lose their jobs.

Golf course grass will turn brown. The Godfather's bad leadership has ruined many businesses of his rich friends. If the Godfathers do not impoverish themselves in order to gain the goodwill of God and the alien beings, the only friends the Godfathers will have are his family members. Maybe, the Godfathers felt that the only true friends that he ever had were his family members. Maybe, the Godfathers thought that all the gangsters that were telling the Godfathers that they loved them were all lying to them. I think gangsters are capable of loving the Godfathers because I think most gangsters love their wives and their children. If the Godfathers do not care whether their gangsters go to hell, I think the Godfathers do not love their gangster friends. If the Godfathers do nothing to deal with the environmental problems of the earth it shows that they do not care about their fellow gangsters or the rest of mankind. If the Godfathers do not forgive David Hashioka, God and the alien beings cannot forgive the Godfathers' past sins. Jesus Christ emphasized the importance of loving your enemies. If the Godfathers kill David Hashioka, they obviously have not forgiven David Hashioka. If the Godfathers only know how to be cruel, destructive, and evil they should not get their way. The Godfathers are not good businessmen. They only think in terms of short-term profitability. If the Godfathers thought in terms of long-term profitability, they would have taken into consideration the environmental needs of the planet earth.

The United States spends more on health care per person than any other country in the world. However, the United States has about the 25th best life expectancy in the world. The United States spends about 20%-50% more in salaries for its doctors than Europeans do. The United States spends about twice as much for medications than Europeans do. The United States spends about 5 times more for diagnostic procedures than Europeans do. According to Oliver Stone if the United States

Congress allowed Medicare to competitively bid for medications, the United States taxpayer could save about $1 trillion. The most important way to control federal government spending is to control the rising cost of health care in the United States. The Republicans and the Democrats have done nothing to control the rising costs of health care in the United States. It is sad that Americans depend on private health care insurance companies to pay for all health care bills. The United States needs a national health care service to take care of all the health care needs of its citizens. This national health care service would be funded by the taxation of all the inhabitants in the United States and all businesses operating in the United States. If we want God to be merciful, this national health care service would pay any expense necessary to save the life of every person living in the United States. People who do not use the national health care service during any given year would be given some type of reward. God does not approve of abortion. The problem with many conservative Christian fundamentalist groups is that they do not support government programs that help take care of poor children whose lives were spared because abortions were prevented. According to Whoopi Goldberg of the television program, The View, one out of every two African American children is born to a family that has no father. According to Yes! magazine 38% of all African American children live in poverty stricken families. According to Yes! magazine, about 34% of all Hispanic American children live in poverty stricken families. 50 % of all foster children in the United States do not graduate from high school. How are these foster children going to find jobs without a high school diploma? I do not think the American taxpayer should be forced to support children born to mothers who are citizens of Mexico who have stayed in the United States for less than 5 years. The United States government should make sure that African American citizens should get jobs before jobs can be given to Latin American immigrants. Employment agencies should not be discriminating against African American citizens. These private employment agencies should not be giving jobs to Mexican immigrants when there are so many African American citizens who need jobs. I do know that many Mexicans would not want to come to the United States if living conditions were acceptable in Mexico. There is an inequitable distribution of wealth in Mexico. According to Ravi Batra the wealthiest 10% of Mexicans benefit from 40% of Mexicos economic output. The poorest 20% of Mexico's citizens receive about 3% of Mexico's economic output. Mexican workers would be paid better if more Mexican workers belonged to unions Rich Mexicans order corrupt Mexican policemen to kill any Mexicans who try to organize new unions in Mexico. For too long in Mexican history a Mexican had to control the most powerful military force in Mexico in order to become President of Mexico. Unfortunately, the formation of powerful political parties came so late to Mexico. It took too long for the first powerful political party, the PRI, the Institutional

Revolutionary Party to form in Mexico. Unfortunately, for too long, the PRI was the only important political party in Mexico. This dominance of one political party in Mexican politics corrupted Mexican government. I think the United States Armed Forces should be withdrawn from many other parts of the world and be used to destroy the control of Mexican drug lords over about 50% of Mexico's land. Mexico needs tourism income badly. Many people would like to visit Mexico, but they are afraid of visiting Mexico because they are afraid of being attacked in Mexico. Many Mexican cities that Americans liked to visit are no longer safe to visit. Cabo San Lucas is still popular and safe to visit, Huge oil deposits were discovered by Mexico's government in 1978. Billions of dollars in oil deposit revenues were stolen from the Mexican government by high ranking government officials. The identity of these corrupt government officials is known. They should be prosecuted. This stolen government revenue could have been used to improve the Mexican economy and make college education more affordable for all Mexican citizens. Public education in Mexico is reasonably good. The problem is that most Mexicans cannot afford to acquire advanced job skill education or college education. The Mexican labor force lacks many job skills. Mexico is a light industry country. Mexico does not have much heavy industry. The Mexican government permits Mexican business to pollute the environment too much. If the Mexican government wants to attract more foreign tourists to Mexico it should chlorinate its drinking water and kill the excessive amounts of germs in its drinking water. Many successful Mexicans can avoid paying taxes by bribing Mexican tax collectors. For too long, Mexican government was lead by elected officials who favored capitalism. Abrador, the former socialist Mayor of Mexico City should be elected President of Mexico. Abrador ran for the presidency of Mexico but lost because he did not participate in a national televised presidential candidate debate. The reason why he did not participate in this national televised presidential candidate debate was that he probably would have been killed had he done so. The people of Mexico should elect Abrador to the presidency of Mexico even if he does no future public campaigning for the presidency. I am afraid it has become so dangerous for Abrador to make any public appearances anymore. In the United States it is essential to obtain the approval of the Trilateral commission before you run for the office of President of the United States. The Trilateral commission is run by rich United States banking families. If you do not get the approval of the Trilateral commission before you run for the office of United States President you will be killed while campaigning for the office. In order to gain the approval of the Trilateral commission you must promise to favor capitalism and oppose communism and socialism. You must always favor the use of money. You can never greatly increase taxes on the wealthy. You are not allowed to break up banks that are too big to fail. The political candidates are forced to promise that if elected

President of the United States that will never break up big multinational corporations. The President of the United States is forced to spend a great deal of the taxpayer's money on weapons research. A presidential candidate promised the Trilateral commission that he or she will never nationalize any industries while President of the United States. The Trilateral Commission demands that the United States government spends a lot of money on the purchasing of weapons and other military equipment each year. It does not matter if you are John Kennedy, Lyndon Baines Johnson, Richard Nixon, Hubert Humphrey, George McGovern, Gerald Ford, Jimmy Carter, Ronald Reagan, George H.W. Bush, George W. Bush or Barack Obama, you must obtain approval from the Trilateral Commission before you try to become President of the United States.

Mexico has wisely limited foreign investment in the development of the Mexican economy, but the Mexican government wasted billions of borrowed dollars on poorly planned major public works projects.

The Democrats and the Republicans should be voted out of the U.S. Congress and U.S. presidency. The Democrats and the Republicans support capitalism. We must vote for candidates of the Green Party, the environmentalist party. We should vote for the Green Party candidate for U.S. president, Mr. Stein. The only Democratic Party candidate for United States president that will be an ethical president is the socialist

U.S. senator from Vermont, Bernie Sanders. Hillary Clinton is pro corporation & pro military. She is no good.

For the last 3 winters there has been little snow in the Sierra Nevada Mountains of California. The state of California gets 90% of its drinking water from snow in the Sierra Nevada Mountains. California gets about 5%-10% of its drinking water from the Colorado River of Arizona. Southern California was a desert until Mulholland brought water by aqueducts from northern California. California has some of the best farmland in the entire world. According to Dr. Isaac Asimov only about 11% of all the land of the entire world is capable of growing crops. Most of the world's land cannot grow crops because it is frozen, lacks water, has too many chemicals in it; has too much salt in it; or because it does not have enough top soil, according to Dr. Isaac Asimov. The United States was the fourth largest wine producing country in the world before the droughts. Only France, Italy and Spain produced more wine than the United States. About 90% of the wine the United States produces comes from California's Central Valley. Without an adequate supply of water California cannot grow much grapes to produce wine. A bottle of champagne from France costs about $70 a bottle. Champagne from California cost a great deal less. Without the help of the alien beings, California will have to build cutting-edge solar-powered ocean water desalination plants along California's coast. Middle class and lower class Californians are taxed heavily already. Rich Californians are going to have to be taxed much more if the desalination plants are going to be constructed. The wealthiest 1% of Californians already provide about 50% of all revenue for California's state government, but they can afford to pay more taxes since the richest 1% of Americans owns about as much wealth as the poorest 95% of Americans. 50% of all Americans depend upon underground drinking water for water. The levels of underground water throughout the United States are at low levels. Many boats cannot travel as far up the Mississippi River as they would like. Many Republicans farm states are located in the Mississippi River Basin. Many southern farm states are experiencing droughts. Many farmers are probably rich enough to retire. The reason why most farmers farm is that they like farming. Without water, millions of acres of American agricultural land will be worthless. I think the United States farmers should support the Green Party, the environmentalist party of the United States. Once the Green Party controls the U.S. Congress, it can force rich Americans to pay a lot more in federal income taxes and it can heavily tax the accumulated wealth of the richest Americans. When the rich are forced to help the poor it will be possible to persuade God to let the alien beings help us. 97% of all the glaciers in the world are decreasing in size.

I am David Ken Hashioka, I was born on January 24, 1956, at the California Lutheran Hospital on Hope Street in downtown Los Angeles, California. In 2015, I am about 5 feet 4 inches tall. I weigh about 150 pounds. My grandparents traveled from Japan to the United States before the year 1920. My dad is Dr. Henry Kenji Hashioka. He is a former optometrist. My mom is May Sakaizawa Hashioka. She was my dad's secretary. I spent my first four years of my life in Pacoima, California in a little house on Remington Street. Pacoima is in the San Fernando Valley. The San Fernando Valley is part of Los Angeles County. As of the year 2015, my dad is 95 years old and my mom is 90 years old. My dad married my mom in the year 1950 in Chicago, Illinois. My dad met my mom at a Japanese Christian Church in Chicago Illinois. I guess my dad was attracted to my mom when he first came to the church because it was so unusual for an attractive woman to be so friendly. My mom was the second woman my dad had ever dated. The first woman my dad had ever dated was my mom's sister, Anna. Anna is an unusually wise woman. My mom is very smart but she is a more submissive person than her sister, Anna. My dad married my mom after an intensive 3 months of courtship. It is usually not a good idea to marry the second woman you ever dated. A man or woman should date many people and obtain a good understanding of people before they decide who to marry. My dad had devoted his life to the study of the biological and physical sciences. He had a very poor understanding of human psychology. He was very interested in military history. He had read much of William Shakespeare's work. You can learn a great deal about human nature by reading William Shakespeare. But, women are such complicated creatures. My mom's wholesome beauty and her warm personality attracted many men. But, very few of the men my mom dated had college degrees. In 1940, only 5% of the United States population had college degrees. In 2015, only about 30% of Americans have college degrees. When my dad met my mom he had earned a college degree in optometry, but he had little money. My dad was born in Fowler California. Fowler is a small farm town located near Modesto, California in California's Central Valley. My mom was born in Long Beach, California. My dad and mom were forced to live in Japanese American Internment camps during World War II. These Internment camps were located in Arkansas. They went to Chicago after World War II was over. But, my dad had served in the United States Army as an optometrist located in an army base in the Panama Canal Zone. My mom was much happier in Chicago than she ever was in California. She felt that the white people in the Midwest were much nicer to the Japanese Americans than the white people in California were. My mom's family was very happy about living in Chicago. She did not want to leave the Midwest to come back to California. But she came back to California soon after marrying my dad because the physician told my dad that his respiratory problems were going to get worse if he stayed in Chicago. Today, the average American family moves once every 7 years.

In other words, if a woman marries she will almost certainly leave her hometown to stay with husband. From Kindergarten-6th grade I went to Darby Avenue Elementary School in Northridge, California. Our home was located on Ludlow Street which was one block away from Darby Avenue Elementary School. My mother would watch us walk down Darby Avenue to the school by looking through one of the windows of the house. Most of my grades were "Cs" when I was going to elementary school. I got some "Bs." The only sign that I was smart was that I had a talent for playing chess. My Dad taught me the game of chess when I was 7 years old. I nearly defeated my Dad in the first and only game of chess I played against him. I was close to defeating my Dad during that game when I made a very bad move and lost the game. My Dad did not play many other board games with me. But Dad played a few very exciting games of Stratego with me. I am very thankful for that. My Dad took me to one professional football game. In this game, the Los Angeles Rams played against the Baltimore Colts, Johnny Unitas, the Baltimore Colts quarterback turned in a Superbowl performance in a regular season game. You cannot expect a professional football quarterback to pass better than Johnny Unitas did that football game I saw. It is almost impossible to prevent a quarterback from completing almost all the passes Johnny Unitas attempted that day when he made so many long and incredibly accurate passes. It takes a great quarterback to lead a football team to victory in a NFL championship game or a Superbowl game. Johnny Unitas is truly one of the greatest football quarterbacks of all time. I was so impressed by Johnny Unitas' performance because I have little throwing ability. Roman Gabriel, the Los Angeles Rams quarterback, is a very talented and handsome quarterback, but he is not a great quarterback like Johnny Unitas. Roman Gabriel enabled the Los Angeles Rams to win most of their football games. That's very impressive. But he could never get the Rams into a NFL championship game. My Dad took me to only one professional basketball game. In this game, the Los Angeles Lakers played against the Milwaukee Bucks. Almost all the points the Milwaukee Bucks scored against the Los Angeles Lakers were made by one player. His name is Kareem Abdul Jabbar. During this game, Kareem Abdul Jabbar demonstrated why he is the highest scoring player in the history of professional basketball. Kareem Abdul Jabbar is 7 feet 2 inches tall. His legs are so long that he can cross the length of the basketball court with a relatively few strides. Kareem scored almost all his points using the same bank shot. There is no defense against such good shooting. The Lakers made no attempt to stop Kareem from scoring. It's amazing what one supremely talented center like Kareem can do for a basketball team offensively and defensively. My Dad took me to about 6 games of professional baseball. In a few of the games, the Los Angeles Dodgers played against the very talented San Francisco Giants. I think the Dodgers defeated the Giants in every game I saw between the two teams. The baseball games in which the Los Angeles Dodgers played against the Cincinnati Reds were the most entertaining baseball games I have ever seen in person. It was amazing how many talented athletes were playing for the Cincinnati Reds baseball team. But it was particularly impressive just how good Johnny Bench, Pete Rose, and Joe Morgan were at playing baseball for the Reds. The rivalry between the Dodgers and the Reds was good for professional baseball. The Reds were definitely better than the Dodgers.

I attended Nobel Junior High School in Northridge, California for 3 years. I received mostly Bs and As at Nobel. Almost all the Cs I received I got in my physical education classes. In elementary school I was the only student who wanted to play chess. At Nobel Junior High School Chess Club, I found other students who wanted to play chess. In my senior year at Nobel, our chess club won the San Fernando Valley Junior High School chess team championship. I played the top board. It was a frustrating experience. I did not lose any games, but I did not win many games either. Most of my games were draws. It was the victories on the lower boards that won the championship for our school. It was very kind of Mrs. Summers-Bosch, a history teacher, to sponsor our chess club. Chess is a wonderful game. But, the best thing about playing chess is being able to meet very intelligent people like Mrs. Summers-Bosch.

According to Mother Jones magazine, about 91% of the fish the United States consumes comes from fish farms in Asia. The fish raised in these fish farms in Asia are not healthy to eat because the fish are raised in water that is badly polluted since the fish are living in overcrowded water. Only 2% of the fish the United States imports from Asia are inspected by the United States government. The Europeans inspect about 50% of all the imported fish they consume. It is clear that there is too much fishing occurring in the world. We have to cut down on our consumption of fish. Worldwide shipped meat should always be salted to stop the meat from being infected with disease. The use of antibiotics to prevent the contamination of meat that is shipped for long distances should be stopped. The constant use of new antibiotics to prevent disease from occurring in shipped meats only causes diseases to develop a resistance to new antibiotics. I would encourage grocery stores to use local-crops whenever they can. The average food product that is sold in the grocery stores at the United States on the average travels about 1500 miles to the store. This excessive amount of traveling wastes a lot of energy and helps pollute the atmosphere. Water is an important ingredient in most of the products sold in our stores. Therefore, large quantities of drinking water are critical to our high living standards. 70% of all United States economic activity is due to consumer spending. About 75% of all U.S. consumer spending involves spending money for the construction, improvement and renting of shelter and the purchasing of goods to put in homes. Obviously, the United States construction industry is a source of many more jobs than the American auto industry. One out of every 10 jobs in the United States is due to the U.S. auto industry. The United States auto industry must stop manufacturing cars that use internal combustion engines that burn gasoline which produces greenhouse gases. New cars should have engines that are powered by compressed air. Compressed air-powered engines have been in existence for quite a while but they were not used because rich Americans were making too much money from selling gasoline to the American public. All cars before 1905 used electric motors to power cars. If the cars of today used electric motors we would not be experiencing worldwide droughts, The Rockefellers convinced the American car manufacturers to install gasoline-consuming internal combustion engines in their cars. The problem with electric motor powered cars is that they require the use of either lithium Ion batteries or nickel metal hydride batteries that can leak toxic chemicals. Hydrogen power has many technical problems. Nitrogen use requires storage tanks that are too big. The jet engine powered commercial airline planes produce too much greenhouse gases. I think many bullet trains that travel over magnetic fields should be built to cross the United States in order to transport large numbers of people over great distances

The construction of bullet train track will create many jobs. It costs about $5 billion to built one mile of subway train tracks. The spending of $5 billion will create about 25,000 jobs. It will take an investment of $100 billion to meet all of the city of Los Angeles' transportation needs.

Many Mexican immigrants are taking jobs away from American construction workers who are United States citizens. Mexican immigrant workers are willing to work for a lot less money than United States citizens because Mexican immigrants are willing to share their apartments or condominiums with other families. Mexican immigrants are willing to live in rental space in garages. American citizens are not willing to do this.

The sad reality is that the richest Americans are destroying the United States economy. From the years 2000-2009, United States multinational corporations fired about 2.9 million United States workers and hired 2.4 million foreign workers, according to Yes! magazine. In earlier times, gangsters use to rob banks with guns. Today, the Italian-American Mafia buys banks and then steals money from them. At the present time, rich gangsters buy enough shares of a company in order to become members of the board of directors of a company. Once they become members of the board of directors, they steal a great deal of money from the company. If I were a stockholder, I would demand that union workers be involved in all the decision making of the company. Union worker involvement in all the decision making of a business prevents the board of directors from stealing large sums of money from the company and the shareholders. According to the Yes! magazine from the years 2000-2009, the German economy had a foreign trade surplus of $2 trillion. According to Yes! magazine from the years

2000-2009, the United States had a foreign trade deficit of $6 trillion. From the years 2000-2009, 21% of all German workers were involved in manufacturing, according to Yes! magazine. From the years 2000-2009, 9% of all United States workers were involved in manufacturing. From 1985-2009, German workers had a 30% increase in wages. During the same period of time, according to Yes! magazine, the American workers only experienced a 5% increase in wages. These facts indicate that the German companies are being operated much better than United States companies because German workers participate in all the decision making at all factories because the German constitution requires all German corporations to involve all German union workers in all the corporate decision making. The big differences between the profitability of German corporations and American corporations indicates strongly that members of United States corporate boards are stealing a great deal of money from many American corporations.

Under a democracy, a citizen cannot assume that an elected official will serve the public's best interests without being pressured by the public. The public must express its views on many political issues to the elected government officials.

In the past, I had often wondered why my mother worried so much. My mother was blessed with beauty, intelligence, and a very spiritual upbringing. She had married a handsome, energetic, sensible, smart, educated, caring man who was a good provider. Now, I realized the reason why my mother worried so much because she had always been very psychic. She had never verbally told me she was psychic. Since she was psychic she knew that almost all the countries of the world were controlled by organized crime families. Being psychic, my mother also knew that her son had been Krishna, Mahavira, Lao-Tzu, Akhenaten Plato, Euclid, Marco Polo, Christopher Columbus, Leonardo da Vinci, Martin Luther, King Henry VIII, Sir Isaac Newton, Augustus Caesar, Alexander the Great, Leif Erickson, King Phillip II of Spain, King Louis XVI of France, Dr. Edward Jenner, Adam Smith, Joseph Lister, Lewenhook, Thomas Jefferson, James Madison, Abraham Lincoln, Benjamin Disraeli, Woodrow Wilson, Dr. Sigmund Freud, John Maynard Keynes, Mao Zedong, Jim Thorpe, Paramanhansa Yogananda, John Kenneth Galbraith, Sir Arthur Conan Doyle, William Shakespeare, Jules Verne, Charles Dickens, Wolfgang Amadeus Mozart, John Lennon, Humphrey Bogart, Henry Fonda, James Mason, Charlie Chaplin, Mark Twain, Lyndon Barnes Johnson, John Fitzgerald Kennedy, Dr. Martin Luther King, Jr., Will Rogers, and Bobby Fischer, and many others in past lives. Being psychic, my mother also knew that the Godfathers of the Italian-American Mafia wanted to kill me. Why? The Godfathers feared I could decrease their wealth greatly. I know that I can't take control of the world away from the organized crime families because there are not enough people to criticize publicly the bad, powerful and rich people of the world. Not enough people want to live the life of a savior, like Jesus Christ. When you criticize publicly the greed of big corporations, and very wealthy people, the Mafia will make it difficult for the protester to earn a living. The Mafia forces your employer to fire you from your job. Basically, you have to be willing to become homeless and risk your life if you want to decrease greatly the number of economic, social, environmental and spirituality problems facing all mankind. Most people are too scared of dying and going to hell to oppose the Mafia. All the big problems facing mankind exist because the organized crime families have too much power and wealth. Rich people think they are wealthy because they work harder and are more talented than most other people. The rich are rich because they own too much of the world's wealth. The rich are rich because the poor people are so poor.

My mother began sending me to psychological therapists when I was a little boy. For a long time I thought my mother was wasting a great deal of money sending me to psychologists and psychiatrists for psychological counseling. I thought I was too young to benefit from psychological counseling. I thought I did not know enough about life to hold a meaningful conversation with a psychological counselor. I agreed to see these therapists because I did not want to upset my sensitive mother. Today, I understand why my mother sent me to all those psychological counselors. In order to be a very spiritual person, it helps to have a very good understanding of psychology. Psychology is the science of mind and behavior. The study of psychology helps you to understand humans, animals, and alien beings living on other planets. Basically, a psychological therapist decides how to treat a patient on the basis on whether the therapist thinks the patient would be happier being himself or being a conformist. Personally, I thought too deeply and knew too much to be happy being a conformist. I always liked being a little different from everyone else. I think it is advantageous to be part of the minority races in the United States. When you are white you tend to want to be like other white people. When you are a minority in the United States, you tend to question more than white people do what is socially acceptable. Therefore, I think racial minorities tend to be more philosophical about life than white people because they are more willing to analyze or question the status quo. Having seen many therapists and having read some very helpful psychology books, I can now figure out what is wrong psychologically with almost anyone no matter how severe their psychological problems. Now, I can understand women better than almost all women do. I am able to understand men better than almost all other men. The late famous psychiatrist Dr. David Viscott had a profound influence on the way I view psychology. Dr. David Viscott claimed that the only way to rid yourself of negative or unwanted emotions is to express it. Dr. Viscott's view differs with the Japanese view on good psychological living. The Japanese claim that you should try to limit or keep under control the expression of your negative or unwanted emotions. I favor Dr. David Viscott's way of dealing with negative or unwanted emotions. Most psychologists and psychiatrists will give advice to their patients based on psychological theory learned in college. A fine therapist will not only provide advice based on psychological theory learned in college but will provide his own insight into your problems. A great therapist should be a friend to his patient. A great therapist should provide advice based on his difficulties in dealing with his own personal relationships.

Personally, I do believe that no one deserves to be swatted, or sent to jail, or put in hell no matter how bad they have been. Jesus Christ was right saying that we should love our enemies. Loving your enemies is necessary to democracy. In order for a democracy to work, people should not kill people they disagree with politically. No friendship or marriage would last if no one was forgiving. If you could prevent a war by forgiving your enemy you should be forgiving. According to actress Selma Hayek, 90% of all the people in U.S. jails come from homes where there was domestic violence. In other words most people go to jail, not because they are bad, but because their parents were bad parents. Parents may give good ethical advice to their children, but their children will only follow the advice of their parents if their parents are good examples. One out of every 99 American citizens has been in jail. This reality is unacceptable because the United States is supposed to be the land of the free. I think dangerous convicts should be put on an island to live instead of being put in a prison or jail to live. Everyone would become rich under communism if humanity had the technology of the advanced alien beings. If we had the technology to convert any form of matter or energy into any other form of matter or energy, we could all be rich under communism and capitalism would no longer be desirable. If the Godfathers impoverish themselves in order to help end poverty, God would allow the advanced alien beings to share all their technology with mankind. There would be no need for humanity to spend much money on scientific research if we had the technology of the advanced alien beings. It would take about 25 to 50 years of international physics research to gain the technology to convert any form of matter or energy into any other form of matter or energy. The key factor is that the United States must greatly decrease what it spends on defense and increase greatly what it spends on useful physics research. We are going to have to gain a better understanding of more subatomic particles. We are going to have to spend more money on the construction of more powerful atom smashers. Salvation is made possible by having the scientific technology to convert any form of matter or energy into any other form of matter or energy. By being able to convert any form of matter or energy into any other form of matter or energy, humans will be able to live forever in their human bodies and escape the harmful judgement of God. By being able to convert any matter or energy into any other form of matter or energy it would be possible to end world poverty and obtain a high standard of living for everyone on the planet earth.

Many people think Hugh Hefner is a shallow human being because he likes beautiful women with big breasts. I do not think Hugh Hefner is a shallow person. Nor, do I think he is a male chauvinist pig. In a past life Hugh Hefner was King David. He slew Goliath and became one of the heroes in the Holy Bible. In another past life Hugh Hefner was Oliver Cromwell of England. As Oliver Cromwell, he defeated the English king and established a democratic parliamentary government in England. This parliamentary government has served as a role model for other parliamentary governments. In another past life, Hugh Hefner was Hannibal. Hannibal was the leading military leader and statesman for the North African city of Carthage. Hugh Hefner respects intelligent women. Hugh Hefner permits his very smart daughter, Christie, to run Playboy enterprises. Hugh Hefner may have started Playboy, but he never ran it. Playboy has always been run by gangsters. Hugh Hefner may pose with the Playmate of the Year, but he does not select the Playmate of the Year. Gangsters select the Playmate of the Year. Hugh Hefner knows that the $100,000 check and the car that is awarded to the Playmate of the Year is a poor type of compensation for the job of being Playmate of the Year, because the Playmate of the Year is a sex slave for gangsters. All the Playboy playmates are sex slaves for gangsters. All famous actors, athletes, comedians, painters, singers, musicians, writers, directors, and fashion models are sex slaves to gangsters. Hugh Hefner feels sorry that all these people are sex slaves, but there is nothing he can do about it.

Like all celebrities, Hugh Hefner gets swatted by gangsters. All Playboy playmates have had sex with so many gangsters that they have no sexual desire for men. Lesbians do not like men to gain sexual pleasure from looking at beautiful women with voluptuous figures, big breasts, and big nipples. But, lesbians think it is alright for women to obtain sexual pleasure from looking at women with voluptuous figures, big breasts, and big nipples.

Most publications are politically correct. The beauty of Playboy magazine is that it is a politically incorrect publication. Playboy magazine refuses to be censored by rich and powerful people. Playboy magazine is the only internationally distributed publication that often interviews politically influential people. The Playboy interview is an ingenious idea from Hugh Hefner. If Playboy magazine asked the right people the right questions it could do more good than even the Holy Bible. Playboy magazine should promote environmental protection, the equitable distribution of wealth and the free flow of information and ideas. Playboy should oppose all censorship. I am sure that there are many politically influential people who have ideas as to how the United States government could be run more effectively.

By publishing interviews with important people Playboy magazine has done much more to help Americans understand the world than the highly censored American television news programs. Barbara Walters does a very poor job interviewing celebrities. She asks celebrities politically correct questions. She avoids asking questions about their political values. She avoids interviewing rock stars. The political thinking of celebrities influences the politics of their fans. Playboy magazine interviewed Fidel Castro, Malcolm X, Dr. Martin Luther King, Jr., Jesse Jackson, Huey Newton, Frank Sinatra, Johnny Carson, Woody Allen, John Lennon, Yoko Ono, Tom Hayden, Jane Fonda, Barbra Streisand, Ralph Nader, Jimmy Carter, John Kenneth Galbraith, John Wayne, and Gore Vidal. The United States richest people do not want the average American to talk about religion and politics with anyone they meet. The rich claim that religion and politics are too personal to talk to complete strangers about. I believe that ethical philosophy and politics is everyone's business. It is important that political and ethical philosophies are compared before people vote in a democratic society. A psychological counselor should understand why people have the ethical values they do have. Basically, a psychological counselor must be a little philosophical about life. The New York Times, The London Times, London's The Guardian, The Los Angeles Times, The Wall Street Journal, Barron's, The Economist, and Time Magazine are important publications but they are not as widely distributed internationally as

Playboy magazine and the Jehovah Witnesses Watchtower magazine. True, almost every country has its own celebrity gossip magazines, but it seems to me that only Playboy magazine and the Jehovah Witnesses' Watchtower magazine are the only internationally available sources of serious idea discussion. The problem with the Jehovah Witnesses' Watchtower magazine is that it does not interview politically influential people like Playboy magazine does.

Frank Sinatra is a very misunderstood celebrity. Frank Sinatra thought that John Kennedy, Robert Kennedy, and Edward Kennedy were political leaders who were doing a great deal of good work to make the United States a good country to live in. Unfortunately, the Kennedy family rejected Frank Sinatra because he had gangsters as friends. I think the Kennedy family should have been more understanding. Frank was raised in the state of New Jersey. Millions of gangsters live in the states of New Jersey and New York. Many of Frank's boyhood friends were the sons of gangsters. Gangsters are often nicer to their wives than men who are not gangsters. Like other people, gangsters need friends. Life can be very lonely without friends. In many ways, friends are more important than money. Hopefully, the woman you are married to is one of your best friends. Obviously, gangsters like to think that their wives are among their best friends. If you want to become a famous entertainer, you have to have gangsters as your friends. The gangsters run the motion picture studios, the television stations, the major music recording companies, the radio stations, the major book publishers, the casinos, and the major night clubs. There are people who say that Frank Sinatra had sex with too many women. Personally, I do not think a man is immoral because he has sex with many women who are not his wives. Frank never forced any of these women to have sex with him. Many of Frank's female fans would have been very disappointed if Frank was not promiscuous. If it was socially acceptable to have sex out of marriage, it would be easier for a nice ugly woman to marry a good man, since it would be alright for a married man to have sex with a beautiful woman who was not his wife. I do not find anything wrong with polygamy. It is better for a nice ugly woman to be one of several wives of one man than to not be married to anybody. 50 women would feel honored if they could be one of the wives of Frank Sinatra, Elvis Presley, Paul McCartney, or Warren Beatty.

Frank Sinatra was an unusually generous person. Frank raised over 100 million 2015 U.S. dollars for charity, during his lifetime. Very few entertainers have been so generous. Jerry Lewis, Marlo Thomas, Michael Jackson, Olivia Newton-John, and Elton John are among the few celebrities that have been as generous as Frank Sinatra.

Walt Disney was a man who had sex with many other women besides his wife. But, I still think Walt led a good, productive life. Disney made us realize how entertaining animated cartoons could be. Walt Disney created Disneyland, the world's most popular amusement park. Whenever I go to Disneyland, I ask myself what is happiness? What makes people happy? What is heaven on earth like? Walt Disney created Walt Disney World in Orlando, Florida. In Walt Disney World, Walt Disney gives us ideas as to how the world of tomorrow should look like. Disney created the Experimental Prototype Community of Tomorrow (EPCOT) for showing mankind what the world of the future could look like.

Gene Roddenberry had sex with many women besides his wife. In my opinion, Gene Roddenberry is the most important writer of fiction of all time. Gene created Star Trek, a science fiction television series, about humanity's voyages into outer space. Before Star Trek, the spiritual outlook for mankind looked very dim. After Star Trek, it became clear that humanity could obtain salvation through international cooperation and by using advanced scientific technology. By using Star Trek transporter room technology, humans could live in their human bodies forever and escape harsh judgement from God. Star Trek made us realize we could develop a better understanding of ourselves and life by studying the cultures of alien worlds.

Gore Vidal said he had sex with over 1000 men and women before he was 25 years old. Gore is one of the few celebrities that publicly attacked the Mafia. Gore is one of the few celebrities who claimed that the United States government does not promote democracy throughout the world, but instead, the United States government tries to control the rest of the world. Gore has made it clear that rich Americans have always tried to tell other Americans what to do. According to Ralph Nader 1500 large corporations totally control what the United States Congress does. The big corporations should not get their way because they want to take good jobs out of the United States. In the last 15 years, 64% of all the new jobs created in the United States were created by community businesses. According to Yes! magazine, there are about 200,000 small businesses in the United States that employ 50% of all United States workers. A small business employs fewer than 500 workers. According to Yes! magazine, if present trends continue, about 48% of all jobs in the United States will be low-paying fast-food restaurant jobs by the year 2040.

The richest people in the world have invested $700 trillion in derivatives. Derivatives are investment tools like stock options. Derivatives make money for investors when the prices of investment assets are manipulated up and down. If $700 trillion were invested in job creating businesses, there would be no unemployment in the world. All the stock on all the stock exchanges all over the world is worth only $61 trillion, according to Class Struggle magazine. Rich Americans create unemployment so that average Americans will be grateful for their jobs.

The way to create jobs is to tax the rich Americans more, not less. If you tax rich Americans less, they invest their money in derivatives and rare art antiques-investments that do not create jobs. The more the federal government taxes rich Americans, the more public infrastructure repair jobs can be created. The public infrastructure must be repaired.

The public infrastructure includes roads, bridges, aqueducts, dams, sewers, sewage water treatment plants, airports, schools, libraries, courthouses, government administration buildings, mass transit systems, beaches, and parks. The more rich Americans are taxed, the more affordable public college education can be made. 80% of America's college students go to public colleges. It is not the amount of farmland or the amount of mineral resources that makes a country prosperous, but it is the talents of the workers that determines the prosperity of a country. One Phd. in the biological and physical sciences can create thousands of jobs. The average graduate with a bachelor's degree is over $20,000 in debt.

President Reagan believed that the way to create jobs is to make the rich richer. President Ronald Reagan lowered the federal personal income tax rate from 70 percent down to 28 percent. He lowered the capital gains tax rate from 28 percent to 20 percent. President Reagan lowered the corporate tax rate from 46 percent to 35 percent. The rich Americans have so successfully evaded taxes over the years that the United States government is deeply in debt. The U.S. dollar is weak. The United States government is so deeply in debt that it could not fight wars in the Middle East without borrowing billions of dollars from the Chinese and Japanese. In exchange for the loan money from the Japanese and the Chinese, the United States government has to maintain a free trade policy that does not permit the United States government to tax any goods that are imported into the United States. Labor costs are usually lower in Japan and China than in the United States. If the U.S. government does not tax imported goods, those imported goods will usually be cheaper than goods made with expensive American labor. The United States free trade policy has cost the United States millions of jobs since it was established in 1973.

The United States did not invade Iraq to get rid of terrorists. The United States did not invade Iraq to get rid of Saddam Hussein. The reasons why the United States invaded Iraq are that it wanted to capture Iraq's oil fields and because rich Americans wanted to sell weapons to the United States Defense Department. The reason why the United States fought the Vietnam War is because wealthy Americans wanted to sell weapons to the Defense Department. The way to get rich in the United States is to sell goods and services to the United States government. The President and the United States Congress have been corrupted by offers of sex and money since the time of President George Washington. Benjamin Franklin said the average American does let logic guide his voting. He said self-interest guides the average voter. Throughout most of United States history, low ethics has guided the average American voter. The rich American has told the average American voter that the way to prosper is to steal land from the American Indian, and exploit the labor of the African American slave. According to Hedrick Smith, the American worker is underpaid. From 1946-1973, United States labor productivity rose 96 percent. From 1946-1973, wages rose 94 percent. From 1973-2011, United States labor productivity rose 80%. From 1973-2011, United States wages only increased a tiny bit. Productivity is output per hour worked. According to the Los Angeles Times, 50% of Los Angeles workers get paid $15 or less an hour, which means they are barely getting by. McDonalds could pay $19 an hour, if they raised the price of a hamburger by $1. McDonald does not want to pay higher wages because they are greedy.

The world is overpopulated. The use of birth control is an absolute necessity. About 900 million people go hungry in the world every day. 85% of the world's people live in poverty.

The world cannot keep functioning the way it has in the past. Today, the Mafia swats all important politicians in the United States. The Mafia swats all celebrities. In the past, the Mafia has swatted leading liberal intellectuals like Ralph Nader, Noam Chomsky, Gloria Steinem, Bette Friedan, Cesar Chavez, Gore Vidal, Dr. Martin Luther King, Jr., Jesse Jackson, President John Kennedy, Senator Robert Kennedy and Senator Ted Kennedy. All people who work for the motion picture studios, television stations, radio stations, major music recording companies & major book publishers get swatted. All the Playboy playmates get swatted. All the fashion models get swatted. Beauty pageant contestants are raped and swatted. The happiest actors do not act in front of a camera or on a stage. The happiest actors are teachers, preachers, and therapists.

The attitude of the two oldest Godfathers is that only gangsters deserve to be happy. If you are not a gangster, you deserve to suffer. If you are good, you deserve to suffer. If the two oldest Godfathers had their way, everyone who went to church would be swatted. One day all the high school female cheerleaders will be lesbians because they will have been raped so much by gangsters. One day almost all females will be lesbians because they have been raped so much by gangsters. One day, all men will be gay because women will no longer want to have sex with men because they have been raped so much by gangsters.

I do not like capitalism because it distributes wealth inequitably. Capitalism tends to concentrate wealth in the hands of a few. If you are very talented, you can be rewarded handsomely under capitalism. If you are average at everything you do, you will be treated badly by capitalism, unless you belong to a union or you are a gangster. Capitalists tend to ignore the costs of polluting the environment. It is the people who own the means of production who get rich under capitalism. Bartering is a very inefficient way of exchanging goods. Under capitalism, money is used to exchange goods and services. The use of money creates many opportunities to distribute wealth inequitably. Under communism, there is no money. All wealth belongs to everyone under communism. All wealth is shared under communism. It is for these reasons that I like communism. According to Oliver Stone, the wealthiest 10% of the world's people control 85% of the world wealth.

I believe that no one should be swatted, imprisoned, or sent to hell no matter how badly they might have behaved. It may seem logical to punish sin. But it was not logic that motivated Jesus Christ to suffer so much in order to help the human race. Jesus Christ helped the human race because he believed in love and forgiveness. Logic is not what motivated Buddha to serve humanity. Buddha was persecuted for about 35 years. Buddha served humanity because he believed in love and forgiveness.

I think human society tries to control people too much. Society should not make people feel guilty about being overweight. If a person is willing to accept the health risks of being overweight, society should not criticize a person for being overweight. It should be socially acceptable for a person to smoke as many cigarettes as he wants to, as long as he accepts the health risk of smoking. It should be socially acceptable to take cocaine or heroin as long as the drug user knows he can handle the problems of drug abuse. It should be socially acceptable for a person to be lesbian, gay, or bisexual. It should be socially acceptable to look at pornography. God is not embarrassed by human nudity. In the eyes of God, humans are always naked anyway. Everyone appears naked to everyone else since almost everyone is psychic any way.

The droughts occurring throughout the United States and the rest of the world are caused by global warming. Global warming occurs when there is too much greenhouse gases like carbon dioxide and methane in the earth's atmosphere. Carbon dioxide is produced when gasoline is burned. All humans and animals produce methane after their bodies digest food. Methane is the second most abundant greenhouse gas in the world. Carbon dioxide is the most abundant greenhouse gas in the world. The more greenhouse gases there are in the earth's atmosphere, the less heat can escape into outer space from the earth's atmosphere. This trapping of heat causes global warming.

Throughout my teenage years, I played basketball, tennis, hide and go seek, 3 dimensional Tic-Tac-Toe, Monopoly, Clue, Risk, Go, and Chess. While I was in junior high school I could beat college students at chess. I liked all kinds of music. Hard rock, Progressive rock, Pop rock, Jazz, country, soul, disco electronic music, folk music, classical music. Playing chess at Granada Hills High School Chess Club was important to me. At one of the Christmas season chess tournaments sponsored by the Piatigorsky Chess Foundation, Granada Hill High School had the most students participating in the chess tournament. Mr. Sam Berman, an English teacher, was the high school chess club sponsor. He taught a class called the Bible as literature. Mr. Sam Berman had the opportunity to accept a document declaring the high school's outstanding participation at the Christmas season chess tournament, Mr. Sam Berman disagreed with Los Angeles Mayor Sam Yorty's politics so he sent me instead to receive the document. The chambers of the Los Angeles Mayor's office were quite beautiful. I do not remember much about meeting Los Angeles Mayor Sam Yorty. But I do remember I was very nervous. I was selected to go to the Los Angeles Mayor's office because I was president of the high school chess club.

I made the honor roll society once while I attended Granada Hills High School. I graduated with low honors in the 1973 Amitian class from Granada Hills High School. The elder chess champion of the high school once asked me why I did not make the honor roll society more often than I did. I told him that I am a slow learner who can only remember what he understands. In order to make the honor roll, it helps to be a fast learner who can remember what he does not understand. You can be good at memorizing information and not be very intelligent. In order to play very good chess you have to understand problems. Memorizing is not understanding. While I was at Granada Hills high school I was the second best chess player at the high school.

After I graduated from Granada Hills high school I went to Pierce Community College in Woodland Hills, California. I made the Dean's List twice while attending Pierce College. My years at Pierce College were lonely, because I seemed to be the only student who was majoring in history. I graduated with an associate's of arts degree in history from Pierce College. I spent the next 35 years doing research and writing this book. I found reading Lester Thurow, Ralph Nader, Robert Heilbroner, John Kenneth Galbraith, Robert Reich, Ravi Batra, Joseph Stiglitz, Jesse Jackson, Barry Commoner, Mortimer Adler, David Viscott and the Holy Bible to be quite helpful in writing my book. If you let the clock limit the amount of time you spend thinking about serious issues you will never become truly wise. You have to make mistakes in order to learn and become wise. If you are too concerned about what others think of you; you will never be willing to make the mistakes that will help you to learn and to become wise. Reading publications like The American Prospect, Yes! Magazine, The Nation, Mother Jones, The Progressive, Class Struggle, The Progressive Populist, and Playboy have also been useful in writing this book.

Someone once asked me if the average person was free under capitalism or under communism? I answered communism. Under capitalism, the amount of money and wealth you have determines how much freedom and rights you have. Under communism, there is no money. All wealth belongs to everyone else. Under communism, you can get what you want or need without money. Under capitalism, according to Oliver Stone the wealthiest 10% of the world's people control 85% of the world's wealth. According to Fidel Castro, 85% of the world's people are poor. According to United States Senator Bernie

Sanders, the wealthiest 1% of Americans owns as much wealth as the poorest 95% of Americans. According to Ravi Batra the wealthiest 1% of Americans owns over 90% of the nonresidential wealth of the United States. According to the Los Angeles Times one out of every 6 Americans lives in poverty under capitalism. Under capitalism, according to the Los Angeles Times 900 million people go hungry every day in the world. Enough food is grown by the world to feed everyone. There are people who are hungry because those people do not have the money to buy the food they need to have.

Men and women are different in many ways. But, both men and women are more influenced by their emotions than by their logical thinking which is good. Most of a human being's decisions should be influenced more by feelings than by logic. What work that you want to do should be determined more by your feelings than by your logic. Your selection of friends should be determined more by your feelings than by your logic. Your choice of hobbies should be determined by your emotions rather than by your logic. Your choices in movies, television shows, and music should be determined by your emotions than by your logic. There is no doubt that the brains of women and men are different. Women are much more emotionally sensitive than men. Women are more guided by their emotions than men are. Men tend to be more result oriented. I think nature made women more guided by emotions than men, because women are supposed to take care of the emotional needs of their children. In order to make a living, men often have to do work that they do not want to do, that is why they are less guided by their emotions than women are. A woman can only enjoy having sex with a man she cares about. Women can only enjoy having sex with a man they think God approves of. On the other hand, men can enjoy having sex with a woman they are physically attracted to even if they do not care about the woman. Men need to have sex more often than women because men easily have erections that give them a great deal of sexual pleasure. Men dance because the women they date like to dance. Since women are more sensitive to everything, they are more sensitive to pain. Women are more fearful of the pain of hell than men are. Women tend to be more spiritual than men are. Women are much more concerned about what other people think of them then men are. Women are very aware of the pain of social rejection. Men are less so. Men tend to accomplish more in life than women because they are willing to take more risks with their reputations than women are. Men are more willing to make mistakes and appear foolish than women are. How can you become an expert without learning from mistakes. You have to appear foolish before you can become truly wise. Women often get upset when their men get interested in other women. But, men should always remember that the woman they marry would probably preferred to marry a famous male singer of love songs like Frank Sinatra, Dean Martin, Elvis Presley, Placido Domingo, Paul McCartney, John Lennon,

George Harrison, Ringo Starr, Neil Diamond, or Brian Wilson. Women tend to be much more interested in drama, art, music, and literature than men are. Men are more interested in the biological and physical sciences than women are. Men tend to be much better at performing mathematics than women are. Men tend to be more interested in how machines work than women are.

In my opinion, the government has a moral obligation to provide a decently rewarding job to everyone who can work. If a person cannot hold a job, the government should be required to provide for his needs. A poor person is a person who does not have all his mental needs, emotional needs, physical needs, and spiritual needs met. There is a limit to how many poor people there are. World poverty can be solved. It is a mental need to require to have purpose in one's life. It is an emotional need to require being loved by somebody else. It is a physical need to require food, clothing, shelter, and health care. It is a spiritual need to require having a good relationship with God.

The problem with this world is that if you want to talk to the President of the United States you have to have the approval of the Godfather first. If you want to talk to the Pope, you have to have the approval of the Godfather. If we are to restore democracy the United States Constitution must be amended so that it is illegal for a private citizen to own a gun. The President of the United States, being the commander-in-chief, can order the U.S. Army and the U.S. Marines to search and seize all guns from private homes. The President should bring many troops home from overseas. We have to disagree with the Godfathers. The Godfathers want us to believe that might makes right. Obviously, only right makes right. The Godfathers want us to think that material things are more important than people. If people thought material things were more important than people, the poor people would not be helped out much. If a person does not help poor people, God will not want to help that person. Sinning is killing yourself to live. Rich people make a lot of money by manufacturing toxic chemicals. In 42 states, the drinking water has at least 100 chemicals. According to Adler, 70% of all the chemicals in the United States are toxic. Many U.S. physicians do not want to think about the health problems caused by pollution.

Public school teachers should be employees of the federal government. Local towns and cities are unwilling to pay teachers decent salaries for teaching. The rich Americans have to pay a lot more in taxes to support public education in the United States. American students are about 25th best in the world in Mathematics and Science. The Chinese graduate tens of thousands more scientists each year than the United States does.

China and Russia are not true communist countries because they use money. They are socialist states. It should be noted that some of the Chinese political leaders are billionaires. The problem with capitalism is that you can get what you want, but you pay a great deal to get it. Whenever you buy a car, you have to pay a great deal of interest on the car loan, the auto insurance, and the automobile maintenance costs. Rich people tend to want to corrupt government officials so that the government can make them richer. When there is government corruption, a lot of people suffer.

www.ingramcontent.com/pod-product-compliance
Lightning Source LLC
Chambersburg PA
CBHW030541290526
45786CB00004B/1804